DESTINATION FRENCH

Illustrated Phrasebook & Travel Information

Anne Gruneberg and
Mike Buckby

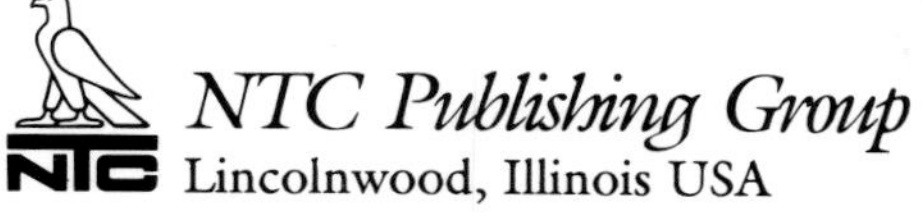
NTC Publishing Group
Lincolnwood, Illinois USA

Book and Tapescript by
Anne Gruneberg
and Mike Buckby

Cassette produced by Merlilyn Harris

Destination French was produced in collaboration with
the Language Teaching Centre at the
University of York

Illustrations by Tony Kerins

Picture credits:
Jennifer Fry: page 77;
Robert Harding: (Explorer/Y. Arthus-Bertrand), page 70;
Image Bank: page 72 (Francisco Hidalgo),
page 73 (Gerard Champlong),
page 74 (Bullaty/Lomeo), page 75 (Grant Faint),
and pages 82-83 (Harald Schoen);
Barrie Smith: pages 71 and 76.

This edition first published in 1995 by Passport Books,
a division of NTC Publishing Group,
4255 W. Touhy Avenue, Lincolnwood, Illinois, USA 60646-1975.

Published in co-operation with BBC Enterprises Limited.

Printed in Hong Kong.

5 6 7 8 9 0 WKT 9 8 7 6 5 4 3 2 1

CONTENTS

HOW TO USE THIS BOOK

WELCOME TO *DESTINATION FRANCE*!

This book is for young people who would like to know about France, French, and the French. There is also a cassette designed for use with the book. But don't be put off if you don't have the cassette, because they can also be used separately. So, whether you're in the library, on the train, or even just walking down the street, using *Destination French* is the perfect way to learn French.

The *Destination French* book

The first part of the book is about the language.
The second part is about the country.
The language section contains:

— some Key Phrases to get you started
— twelve useful situations/**unités**
— a list of additional **words** and **phrases**
— useful slang expressions

The second section on life in France contains:

— maps of France
— information on France, the country
— information on French life style
— information on French in the world

You can start with the first **unité** and work through the book. You can also use the **unités** in any order. Each **unité** is made up of:

Key Phrases

They will help you to understand the

conversations. Try learning as many as you can. When you think you know all of them, cover the French with a piece of paper and write on it the French phrase you have covered up. Then ask a friend to say the English and you give the French.

Conversations

Read them and check if you understand them. They'll help you to say what you want in France.

Find Out More

Here you will find information about new words and phrases.

Over To You

This is a very important section where you will be able to check what you've learned through games and short dialogues.

Answers

Only look at the answers once you've done all the games! There is space in the book for your answers and drawings, but you could do them on some spare paper to keep the book clean.

There is a list of additional words and phrases after the **unités**. They are related to the twelve units and arranged in topics like *Shopping*, *Spare time*, etc. You will also find sections on *Numbers*, *Days*, *Months*, *Time*, *Weather*, *Colors*, *Clothes sizes*, *Weights and measures*, and *Money*. At the end of this section there is a list of colloquial or "slang" expressions used mainly by young people so you can join in their conversations more quickly.

All these words will help you to improve your vocabulary, and test yourself.

The second section of the book tells you about the French, how they live, what you can do and cannot do when in France, and gives you information about the country itself so that you'll feel confident when you arrive.
You'll also find a map showing in which countries French is spoken.

The *Destination French* cassette

The cassette contains the twelve **unités** from the book.
Each **unité** contains:

Écoutez et répétez. This is a list of key phrases for you to listen to and repeat. You can look at them on the relevant pages of this book as you do so.

Trouvez le mot. You hear some French words and phrases. They are grouped according to the sounds they contain. Point to them in the book and keep practicing until you can repeat them all at the same rhythm as the tape.

Conversations. Listen to them as you read them. Stop the tape after each sentence. Repeat it. Play the conversation again and read it aloud with the tape. Then read the conversation aloud once more without the tape.

Écoutez et comprenez. Here you can practice understanding what French people say.

À vous maintenant. You join in one or two conversations as if you really were in France or with French people.

TO GET YOU STARTED

Bonjour and welcome to the French language. You might not yet know any words of French so here is a list to help you get started.

Bonjour madame / monsieur	Hello (to a woman / man)
Bonsoir	Good evening
Bonne nuit	Good night
Au revoir	Goodbye
À demain	See you tomorrow
À bientôt	See you soon
S'il vous plaît	Please
Pardon	Excuse me
Je suis désolé(e)	I'm sorry
Merci beaucoup	Thank you very much
De rien	Don't mention it
Oui	Yes
Non	No
Je ne comprends pas	I don't understand
Je ne sais pas	I don't know
Vous pouvez m'aider?	Can you help me?
J'ai un problème	I've got a problem
Je suis perdu!	I'm lost!
Vous pouvez l'écrire?	Can you write it down?
Vous pouvez répéter?	Can you repeat?
Plus lentement	More slowly
Et	And
Aussi	Too, also
Bon	So, well
Mais	But
Avec	With
Comment ça va?	How are you?
Comment allez-vous?	How do you do?
Ça va bien	I'm fine
Un	One
Deux	Two

(see page 61 for a full list of numbers)

FINDING THE WAY

When you arrive in a town, **une ville**, head for the downtown, **le centre-ville**: here you'll find the tourist information bureau, **l'office de tourisme**. It's usually indicated by this sign: [i] . It's often located near the church, **l'église**, on a square, **la place**, with its cafés, **les cafés**, and restaurants, **les restaurants**.

KEY PHRASES

Pardon, madame / monsieur	Excuse me (talking to a woman / man)
Où est l'office de tourisme?	Where is the tourist office?
Où est la plage / le cinéma / le camping?	Where is the beach / the movie theater / the campsite?
Prenez la première / deuxième rue	Take the first / second street
À droite / À gauche	On the right / On the left
Allez tout droit	Go straight ahead
Près du café	Near the café
Après la poste	After the post office
Tournez à gauche	Turn left
C'est loin?	Is it far?

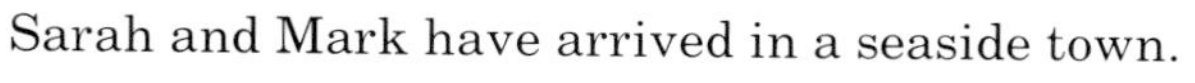

Sarah and Mark have arrived in a seaside town.

Pardon madame, où est l'office de tourisme, s'il vous plaît?
Prenez la première rue à droite.
A droite, près du café?
Oui, et l'office de tourisme est après la poste.
Merci, madame.
Café
Bar

Mark wants to go for a swim right away.

Pardon monsieur; où est la plage, s'il vous plaît?
Après le cinéma, tournez à gauche.
Après, c'est loin?
Non allez tout droit; la plage est après le camping.
Merci, monsieur.

Find Out More

- *The* is **le**, **la**, **l'** or **les**. The easiest is to learn it with the word: **l'**office de tourisme, **le** cinéma, **la** plage, **les** restaurants.
- Here are some more important directions you might have to understand:
  Allez jusqu'aux feux (Go to the lights).
  Allez jusqu'au bout de la rue (Go to the end of the street).
  Traversez le pont / la place (Cross the bridge / the square).
- **La rue** is *the street*. There are other ways of naming streets: **l'avenue**, **le boulevard** (these are wider than a street).

Over To You

1. Try to untangle this line. It'll give you the names of eight different places in a town. Find them and write them all out.

restaurantpostebanquecaféplagecamping cinémapont

2. Ask the way to these different places.

Example: **Pardon monsieur, où est le café?**

____________________ ?

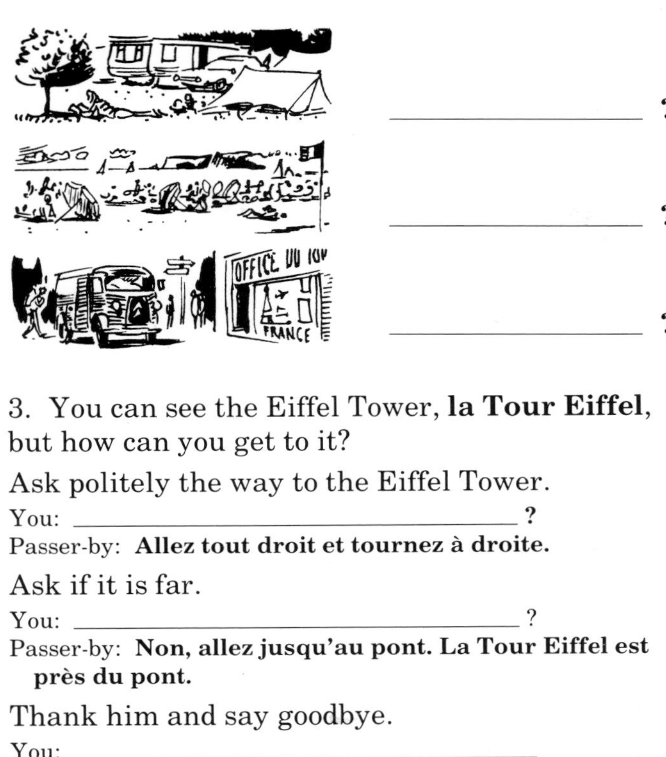

_______________ ?

_______________ ?

_______________ ?

3. You can see the Eiffel Tower, **la Tour Eiffel**, but how can you get to it?

Ask politely the way to the Eiffel Tower.

You: ______________________________ ?

Passer-by: **Allez tout droit et tournez à droite.**

Ask if it is far.

You: ______________________________ ?

Passer-by: **Non, allez jusqu'au pont. La Tour Eiffel est près du pont.**

Thank him and say goodbye.

You: ______________________________

ANSWERS

1. **Restaurant; poste; banque; café; plage; camping; cinéma; pont.**
2. **Pardon monsieur, où est le cinéma?**
   Pardon monsieur, où est le camping?
   Pardon monsieur, où est la plage?
   Pardon monsieur, où est l'office de tourisme?
3. **Où est la Tour Eiffel, s'il vous plaît? C'est loin? Merci. Au revoir, monsieur.**

DRINKS AND SNACKS

In a café people can order many drinks, soft drinks or alcoholic drinks, warm or cold. If you're hungry you can have snacks, ice cream, or cakes. Often the waiter or the waitress is busy, so don't hesitate to call him/her: **Monsieur, s'il vous plaît!** or **Madame, s'il vous plaît!**

KEY PHRASES

Vous désirez?	What would you like?
Un Coca	A Coke
Un croque-monsieur	A toasted cheese and ham sandwich
Un sandwich au pâté	A pâté sandwich
Il y a des sandwichs au saucisson / au jambon	There are salami / ham sandwiches
Un café	A coffee (black)
Un crème	A coffee with milk
J'ai faim	I'm hungry
Je voudrais une omelette et des frites	I'd like an omelette and fries
Comme boisson?	For a drink?
Un jus d'orange	An orange juice

Sarah and Mark are with their friend Pascal in a café.

Bonjour mademoiselle. Vous désirez?

Un coca et un croque-monsieur, s'il vous plaît.

Vous avez des sandwichs au pâté?

Non, il y a des sandwichs au saucisson et au jambon.

Un sandwich au saucisson et un café, s'il vous plaît.

Mark is hungry.

J'ai faim. Je voudrais une omelette avec des frites.
Et comme boisson?
Un jus d'orange.

Find Out More

- *A* is **un** or **une**. The easiest thing is to learn **un** or **une** with the word: **un** coca, **une** omelette. To say "some" you use **des**: **des** frites, **des** glaces, **des** sandwichs.
- **Un café** means the place (a café) or the drink (a coffee). When you ask for **un café** you'll get a small black coffee. If you want milk in it you ask for **un crème**.
- Here are a few more drinks or snacks you might like to have:

un Schweppes (tonic water), **un Orangina** (orange soda), **une limonade** (lemon soda), **une crêpe** (pancake), **un hot-dog, une tarte** (tart), **un thé au lait** (tea with milk), **un thé au citron** (tea with lemon).

For a more complete list see *Eating and drinking* on page 56.

- The tip, **le pourboire**, is always included in the bill.

For more information on café life see page 81.

Over To You

1. What is Mark saying to the waiter?

Example: **Un thé, s'il vous plaît.**

des frites, s'il vous plaît

un sandwich au pate s'il vous plaît

un coca s'il vous plaît

2. You go to a café. What will you say?

Call the waitress politely.

You: Madem s'il vous plaît

Waitress: **Oui, vous désirez?**

Ask for a toasted cheese and ham sandwich.

You: un croque-monsieur

Waitress: **Et comme boisson?**

Ask for an orange juice.

You: un jus d'orange

3. Circle six words related to drinks and snacks in the grid.

A Z C O C A L O
E N A D L Z V R
L I F R I T E S
P A É M P A T S
T U N B X R O M
D O U Z J T H É
O C R E P E B M

A Z C O C A L O
E N A D L Z V R
L I F R I T E S
P A É M P A T S
T U N B X R O M
D O U Z J T H É
O C R E P E B M

ANSWERS

1. **Des frites, s'il vous plaît; Un sandwich au fromage, s'il vous plaît; Une limonade s'il vous plaît.**
2. **Madame, s'il vous plaît! (Je voudrais) un croque-monsieur et un sandwich au jambon. Un jus d'orange.**

SHOPPING FOR CLOTHES

French people like buying clothes and they enjoy dressing well. So you'll find lots of shops offering a wide range of clothes, **les vêtements,** and shoes, **les chaussures.**

KEY PHRASES

Je voudrais essayer le tee-shirt avec la Tour Eiffel	I'd like to try on the T-shirt with the Eiffel Tower
Quelle taille faites-vous?	What size are you?
Quelle pointure faites-vous?	What shoe size are you?
Je fais un 8 (américain)	I'm a size 8 (American)
Voilà une taille 2	Here is a size 2
Il ne me va pas	It doesn't fit me
Il est trop petit/grand	It is too small/big
Les chaussures blanches en vitrine	The white shoes in the window
Je ne sais pas	I don't know
Essayez un 41	Try size 41
Les baskets vous vont?	Do the tennis shoes fit you?
Elles me vont bien	They fit me well
Ces vêtements sont super!	These clothes are great!

Sarah and Mark are shopping, **ils font des courses**. Sarah sees a nice T-shirt to buy.
Bonjour, je voudrais essayer le tee-shirt avec la Tour Eiffel.
Quelle taille faites-vous?
Je fais un 8.
Alors, voilà une taille 2 . . .
Désolée, il ne me va pas, il est trop petit.
575f
Mark is more interested in shoes.
Et moi, je voudrais les baskets blanches en vitrine.
Quelle pointure faites-vous?
Je ne sais pas. Je fais un 9 anglais.
Essayez un 41 . . . Elles vous vont?
Oui, elles me vont bien, elles sont super!
AVIA 51F

Find Out More

- **Je voudrais essayer** is *I'd like to try on*. Feel free to try whatever you like and to walk out without buying if you don't like the clothes or you find them too expensive. For more information on this see page 89–90.
- **Quelle taille faites-vous?** refers to clothes. You will also hear **Quelle est votre taille?**
- **Quelle pointure faites-vous?** refers to shoes. You will also hear **Quelle est votre pointure?**
- **Je fais un 8** is *I am a size 8* (for clothes sizes see page 63).
- **Un tee-shirt** is borrowed from the English language. Here are a few more: **un sweat-shirt**, **un jean**, **un short**. You will need to know a few more French words: **un pantalon**, a pair of pants; **un pull**, a sweater; **une jupe**, a skirt; **une robe**, a dress; **un maillot (de bain)**, a bathing suit (for more clothes see *Shopping* on page 60).

Over To You

1. Fill in the missing vowels. Then say what Sarah is asking to try on.

Example: lx txx-shxrt

Je voudrais essayer le tee-shirt.

lxs bxskxts

lx pxll

lx rxbx

2. Fill in the answers to this dialogue. You will find all the words for the answers scattered around the question.

Monsieur s'il vous plaît?

essayer Je le tee-shirt. voudrais

____

Quelle taille faites-vous?

10 américain un fais Je

____

Voilà une taille deux.

pas. ne va me Il

____

— Il est trop grand?

revoir, au Oui, monsieur.

____

3. What is Doug saying about his shoes?

elles me vont Ces bien, sont baskets super.

ANSWERS

1. **Je voudrais essayer les baskets; je voudrais essayer le pull; je voudrais essayer la robe.**
2. **Je voudrais essayer le tee-shirt; Je fais un 10 américain; Il ne me va pas; Oui, au revoir, monsieur.**
3. **Ces baskets me vont bien; elles sont super.**

SOMEWHERE TO STAY

When in France, you might be staying with your parents in a hotel, **un hôtel**, with friends in a youth hostel, **une auberge de jeunesse**, or at a campsite, **un camping**. Campsites are very popular in France and there is usually one even in a small town.

KEY PHRASES

Vous avez de la place?	Have you got room?
Vous êtes combien?	How many of you are there?
Un adulte/un jeune	An adult/a young person
Deux tentes	Two tents
Vous restez combien de temps?	How long are you staying?
Une nuit/jusqu'au deux juillet	One night/until July 2nd
Un emplacement	A place, a site (e.g., for a tent)
On peut manger ici?	Can we eat here?
Il y a une cafétéria/ un supermarché/ un magasin	There is a cafeteria/ supermarket/shop
Ouvert(e)/fermé(e)	Open/Closed
Jusqu'à dix heures	Until 10 o'clock
Où sont les douches?	Where are the showers?

Mark and Sarah arrive at a campsite.

Bonjour madame. Vous avez de la place?

Vous êtes combien?

Deux jeunes et deux tentes.

Vous restez combien de temps?

Quatre nuits, jusqu'au deux juillet.

Emplacement huit, s'il vous plaît.

Sarah wants to know about more practical things.

On peut manger ici?

Oui, il y a une cafétéria ouverte jusqu'à dix heures.

Et il y a un magasin?

Il y a un supermarché près des douches.

Find Out More

- **La place** here means room. **Vous avez de la place?** Do you have room? **Une place** can also be a square, **place de la Concorde**, or a seat on a train, in a theater or at a concert: **J'ai une place pour le concert de Madonna**.
- Numbers: **deux juillet**, **emplacement dix**, **quatre heures**.

See *Days and Months* on page 62, *Numbers* on page 61, and *Time* on page 62.

- When you are in a hotel you ask for a room, **Vous avez une chambre?** You might have breakfast, **le petit déjeuner**.

Over To You

1. On the left is a form, **une fiche**, that the receptionist gives you when you arrive at the campsite. Can you guess what the French words mean? Now it's your turn to fill in the form on the right.

NOM:
PRÉNOM:
PROFESSION:
ADRESSE:

NATIONALITÉ:
NUMÉRO DE PASSEPORT:
DATE D'ARRIVÉE:
SIGNATURE:

NOM: ______________
PRÉNOM: ______________
PROFESSION: ______________
ADRESSE: ______________
____

NATIONALITÉ: ______________
NUMÉRO DE PASSEPORT: ______________
DATE D'ARRIVÉE: ______________
SIGNATURE: ______________

2. Can you match the following questions and answers?

(1) **Vous êtes combien?**
(2) **Vous restez combien de temps?**
(3) **On peut manger ici?**
(4) **Où est le supermarché?**
(5) **Votre nom, s'il vous plaît**

(a) **Sarah / . . .**
(b) **Nous sommes quatre**
(c) **Deux nuits**
(d) **Il y a une cafétéria**
(e) **Près des douches**

3. You arrive at a campsite in Normandy.

Say hello to the receptionist and ask if there is a space.

You: ______________________________?
Receptionist: **Pour combien de personnes?**

Say you are three young people.

You: ______________________________
Receptionist: **Vous restez combien de temps?**

Say four nights, until July 10th.

You: ______________________________

Ask if you can eat here.

You: ______________________________?
Receptionist: **Oui, il y a une cafétéria.**

ANSWERS
2. **1b; 2c; 3d; 4e; 5a.**
3. **Bonjour, madame. Vous avez de la place? Nous sommes trois jeunes. Quatre nuits, jusqu'au 10 juillet. On peut manger ici?**

MAKING FRIENDS

Whether you are at a campsite, in a youth hostel, or on the beach, you're bound to be surrounded by young French people you'd love to talk to. Here are a few useful expressions to help you join in their conversations.

KEY PHRASES

Tu es anglais(e)/ américain(e)?	Are you English/ American?
J'habite à . . .	I live in . . .
Tu t'appelles comment?	What's your name?
Je m'appelle . . .	My name is . . .
Tu as quel âge?	How old are you?
J'ai douze ans	I'm 12
Et toi?	What about you?
C'est une copine / un copain	It's a friend (girl/boy)
Salut, les filles!	Hello, girls!
Comment ça va?	How are you?
Voici mon frère / ma soeur	This is my brother / my sister
Tu es en vacances ici?	You're on vacation here?

Sarah is on the beach next to Arlette, a French girl. Arlette invites her to play ball.

Fabien, Arlette's brother, wants to join in.

Find Out More

- Saying **tu** or **vous**: you say **tu** to young people of your age and **vous** to adults you don't know very well. **Tu as quel âge? Vous êtes en vacances?**
- Adjectives. **Sarah est américaine**. The ending is with an **e** because it is feminine. Here are a few more nationalities worth knowing: **espagnol** (Spanish), **français** (French), **allemand** (German), **italien** (Italian), **anglais** (English), **australien** (Australian), **japonais** (Japanese).
- **Salut** is a more relaxed way of saying either **bonjour** or **au revoir** (good bye).

See *Greetings* on page 93.

Over To You

1. Fill in the missing sentences from the information given in the passports. The first one has been done for you.

NOM: Barks **PRÉNOM:** Peter **ÂGE:** 13 **ADRESSE:** Bradford	**NOM:** Courtot **PRÉNOM:** Léa **ÂGE:** 12 **ADRESSE:** Lyon	**NOM:** Martinez **PRÉNOM:** Luis **ÂGE:** 14 **ADRESSE:** Barcelone
Je m'appelle Peter Barks	____________	____________
J'ai 13 ans	____________	____________
J'habite à Bradford	____________	____________
Je suis britannique	____________	____________

2. You are by the swimming pool, **la piscine**, and you try to talk to a French boy. Say hello and tell him your name.

You: Salut Je m'appelle Isabelle

Ask what his name is.

You: tu t'appelles comment?

Fabien: **Je m'appelle Fabien.**

Ask if he's on vacation here.

You: Tu es en vacances ici?

Fabien: **Oui, et toi?**

Say yes, you are and say where you live. Ask how old he is.

You: Oui, J'habite a NJK. Tu as quel age?

Fabien: **J'ai 14 ans. Et toi?**

Tell him how old you are.

You: J'ai 13 ans

3. What is Fabien asking Sarah? And what is she replying? You might need a mirror to help you!

Tu es en vacances ici?

Oui, je suis au camping.

ANSWERS

1. **Je m'appelle Léa Courtot. J'ai 12 ans. J'habite à Lyon. Je suis française. Je m'appelle Luis Martinez. J'ai 14 ans. J'habite à Barcelone. Je suis espagnol.**
2. **Bonjour, je m'appelle . . . Tu t'appelles comment? Tu es en vacances ici? Oui. J'habite à . . . . Tu as quel âge? J'ai . . . ans.**
3. **Tu es en vacances ici? Oui, je suis au camping.**

SPARE TIME

When you're on vacation, you like doing things in the evening. Perhaps you like staying in and playing games or watching TV. Perhaps you prefer going out. Here are a few phrases to help you answer if you're asked about your plans for the evening.

KEY PHRASES

Qu'est-ce qu'on fait ce soir?	What shall we do this evening?
Tu veux regarder la télé?	Would you like to watch TV?
Je préfère sortir	I'd prefer to go out
J'adore danser, mais c'est cher	I love dancing but it's expensive
Qu'est-ce qu'il y a au cinéma?	What's on at the movies?
Il y a un très bon film	There's a very good film
Tu veux aller au cinéma?	Do you want to go to the movies?
À quelle heure?	At what time?
À vingt-deux heures	At 10 P.M.
C'est trop tard / tôt	It's too late / early
Il y a aussi un concert gratuit sur le port	There's a free concert at the harbor
On va faire un tour?	Shall we go out for a while?
D'accord	O.K.

Sarah is at Arlette's house. They're deciding what to do in the evening.

Qu'est-ce qu'on fait ce soir?

Tu veux regarder la télé?

Non, je préfère sortir; j'adore danser.

Il y a une discothèque, mais c'est cher.

Qu'est-ce qu'il y a au cinéma?

Arlette's brother, Fabien, joins them.

Il y a un très bon film au cinéma Rex.

Oui, mais c'est à vingt-deux heures; c'est trop tard!

Il y a aussi un concert gratuit sur le port.

On va faire un tour?

D'accord!

Find Out More

- **La télévision** is referred to as **la télé**.

In the same way, **le cinéma** is often called **le ciné**. In France, there are six TV channels (see *TV and radio* on page 89).

- **La discothèque** is usually for people aged 18–30 as it's quite expensive and starts late (discos don't open until 10:30–11:00 P.M.).
- **C'est cher** means it's expensive. To say it's cheap, you'll say it's not expensive: **Ce n'est pas cher**.
- **Un film** is a movie. When buying film for your camera, ask for **une pellicule**.
- **On va faire un tour** is a very useful sentence to say you're going out for a while to look around or to see what's going on. It can be for a drink, for a walk, for a drive, to meet friends, etc.

Over To You

1. Arlette is suggesting different activities for tonight. Can you provide the right question for each suggestion? The first one has been done for you.

2. Answer the following questions with the help of these signs.

−	+	+ +	+++
je n'aime pas	j'aime bien	j'aime beaucoup	j'adore

Tu veux sortir ce soir?	+	Oui, j'aime bien sortir.
Tu veux aller au cinéma?	−	____________
Tu veux danser?	+++	____________
Tu veux aller au concert?	++	____________

3. You'd like to know what Arlette's plans are. Ask her what you should both do tonight.

You: ______________________________?

Arlette: **Tu veux aller au cinéma?**

Ask what's on at the movies.

You: ______________________________?

Arlette: **Il y a un bon film à vingt-deux heures.**

Say it's late. You'd prefer to go out for a while.

You: ______________________________

Arlette: **On va sur le port?**

(Say O.K.)

You: ______________________________

ANSWERS

1. Arlette says: **Tu veux aller au cinéma? Tu veux aller au concert? Tu veux regarder la télé?**
2. **Non, je n'aime pas aller au cinéma. Oui, j'adore danser. Oui, j'aime beaucoup aller au concert.**
3. **Qu'est-ce qu'on fait ce soir? Qu'est-ce qu'il y a au cinéma? C'est tard, je préfère faire un tour. D'accord.**

SHOPPING FOR FOOD

Food is a very important thing for French people. So, you won't starve and you'll find lots of places to buy food: the bakery, **la boulangerie**, the delicatessen, **la charcuterie**, the grocery store, **l'épicerie**, or the market, **le marché**. There are also supermarkets, **les supermarchés**, where food is usually cheaper, but they are rarely downtown.

KEY PHRASES

Je voudrais une baguette	I'd like French bread
Avez-vous des croissants?	Do you have any croissants?
Voilà	Here you are
Et avec ça?	Anything else?
Je vais prendre deux gâteaux	I'll take two cakes
Lesquels?	Which ones?
Une tarte aux pommes	An apple tart
Ça fait combien?	How much is that?
Un kilo d'abricots	A kilo of apricots
Quatre tranches de jambon	Four slices of ham
C'est tout?	Will that be all?
Non, une bouteille d'eau	No, a bottle of water

Mark wants to buy food for a picnic. He goes to the bakery.

Bonjour madame, je voudrais une baguette et deux croissants.

Voilà, et avec ça?

Deux gâteaux, s'il vous plaît.

Lesquels?

Deux tartes aux pommes. Ça fait combien?

Quarante francs.

It's Sarah's turn to ask in the grocery store.

Je vais prendre des abricots.

Combien, un kilo?

Oui, et quatre tranches de jambon.

Voilà, c'est tout?

Non, une bouteille d'eau s'il vous plaît.

Find Out More

- **La baguette** is the most popular bread in France. It has to be eaten fresh. Bakers usually make them twice a day (more types of bread and cakes in *Eating and Drinking* on page 56).
- **Ça fait combien?** means How much is it? You can also say: **C'est combien?** How much does it cost? **Ça coûte combien?**
- **Un kilo d'abricots:** a kilo is just over two pounds. You buy fruit and vegetables by the kilo or the pound, **la livre**. See *Weights and Measures* on page 63.
- **Les abricots:** apricots are common in summer. Here are some other fruits: **des pêches** (peaches), **des poires** (pears), **des nectarines** (nectarines), **des bananes** (bananas), **des oranges** (oranges). See *Eating and Drinking* on page 56.
- **Quarante francs:** see *Numbers* on page 61, and for coins and bills see *Money* on page 63 and *Banks* on page 79.

Over To You

1. How would you ask for these items in a shop?

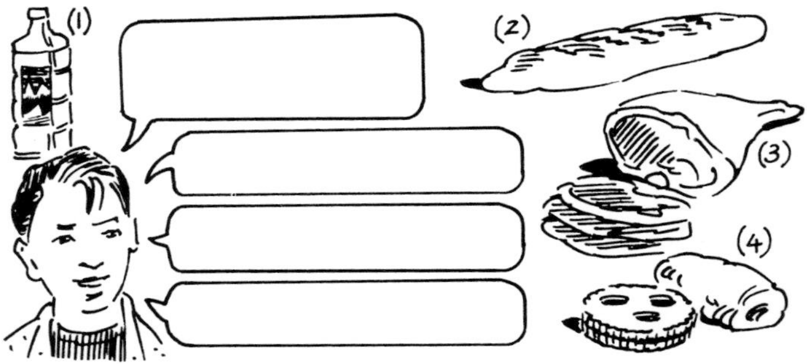

2. You're buying some fruit at the market. Ask for a kilo of apples and some apricots.

You: ______________________________

Man: **Voilà les pommes. Et les abricots, combien?**

Ask for a pound of apricots.

You: ______________________________

Man: **C'est tout?**

Say yes and ask how much it is.

You: ______________________________?

Man: **Quarante-et-un francs en tout.**

3. Do you recognize these fruits?

Now it's your turn to draw these items!

une poire **un gâteau** **une pomme**

ANSWERS

1. **Je voudrais une bouteille d'eau, s'il vous plaît; une baguette; trois tranches de jambon; deux gâteaux.**
2. **Je voudrais un kilo de pommes et des abricots. Je voudrais une livre d'abricots. Oui, c'est combien? / Ça fait combien?**
3. **banane; orange; pêche; abricot**

KEEPING IN TOUCH

If you want to send a postcard to friends or to your family you'll have to buy stamps, **des timbres**. If you want to phone home, you go to a phone booth, **une cabine téléphonique**.

KEY PHRASES

Je voudrais un timbre	I'd like a stamp
Donnez-moi une télécarte à cinquante unités	Give me a 50-unit phonecard
Je prends cinq cartes postales	I'll take 5 postcards
Téléphoner	To phone
Il y a une cabine automatique en face	There is an automatic phone booth across from here
Comment ça marche?	How does it work?
Vous décrochez	You pick up the receiver
Vous mettez la carte	You put the card in
Vous faites le dix-neuf	You dial 19.
Quel est le code?	What is the code?
Quarante-quatre	44
Ensuite, vous faites votre numéro	Then you dial your number
Ça fait soixante-douze francs	That comes to 72 francs

Mark is buying stamps at a tobacco store.
Je voudrais cinq timbres, s'il vous plaît.
Voilà.
Et donnez-moi une télécarte.
À cinquante unités?
Oui, et je prends cinq cartes postales.
Ça fait soixante-douze francs.
SAMEDI 1er Juin
35 MILLIONS !!
Now Sarah wants to phone her parents.
Je voudrais téléphoner.
Il y a une cabine automatique en face.
Comment ça marche?
Vous décrochez, vous mettez la carte et vous faites le dix-neuf pour l'international.
Quel est le code pour la Grande-Bretagne?
Quarante-quatre. Ensuite, vous faites votre numéro.

Find Out More

- **Un timbre**: stamps are at the same price for any country in the European Community (EC).
- **La Grande-Bretagne**: countries start with **le**, **la**, **les** or **l'**: **la** France, **l'**Espagne, **les** Etats-Unis. **la CE** means Communauté Européene (the EC).
- **Donnez-moi** means Give me. It's another way of asking for something, like **Je voudrais** (I'd like . . .) or **Vous avez . . .?** (Do you have . . .?).
- **Une télécarte**: (see *Telephones* on page 85).
- **Comment ça marche?** How does it work? This is a very useful question to remember as it can apply to a lot of things: phones, CD players, ovens, showers, etc.
- **Faire un numéro**: to dial a number.

Over To You

1. Read the sentences below. If it is a sentence you could use to send a postcard, write CP in the box. If it is a sentence you could use to make a phone call, write T in the box.

(a) **Je prends une télécarte.** ☐

(b) **Donnez-moi un timbre.** ☐

(c) **Deux cartes postales, s'il vous plaît.** ☐

(d) **À cinquante unités.** ☐

(e) **Comment ça marche?** ☐

(f) **Quel est le code?** ☐

2. Now make up a conversation which includes, in any order, the six sentences from question 1.

3. You're at the tobacco store.

Tobacconist: **Vous désirez?**

Ask him to give you ten stamps.

You: ______________________________

Tobacconist: **Voilà dix timbres.**

Say you'd like a 50 unit phone card.

You: ______________________________

Tobacconist: **40 F. C'est tout?**

Ask for four postcards.

You: ______________________________

Ask how much it is.

You: ______________________________?

Tobacconist: **Soixante-douze francs.**

ANSWERS

1. **(a) T; (b) CP; (c) CP; (d) T; (e) T; (f) T.**
2. **Un exemple de dialogue avec les six phrases:**
   — Bonjour, monsieur. Deux cartes postales, s'il vous plaît.
   — Voilà.
   — Et donnez-moi deux timbres.
   — Voilà, c'est tout?
   — Je voudrais téléphoner. Je prends une télécarte.
   — À cent vingt unités?
   — Non, à cinquante unités.
   — Il y a une cabine en face.
   — Comment ça marche?
   — Vous faites le dix-neuf et le code de la Grande-Bretagne, 44.
3. **Donnez-moi dix timbres s'il vous plaît. Je voudrais une télécarte à 50 unités. Je voudrais quatre cartes postales, s'il vous plaît. Ça fait combien?/C'est combien?**

UNITÉ NEUF

GETTING AROUND

When traveling in France you might go on the subway (**le métro**) in Paris or Marseille, or you can go on the bus (**le bus**) in every town. When traveling from one place to another you may go by train (**le train**) or by coach (**le car**).

KEY PHRASES

Je voudrais un ticket	I'd like a ticket
Combien?	How many? / How much?
Un carnet	A book of tickets
Pour aller à Montparnasse, s'il vous plaît?	How do I get to Montparnasse?
C'est quelle direction?	Which direction is it?
Vous prenez la ligne numéro quatre	Take line number 4
C'est direct	It's direct
Je voudrais un aller pour Paris	I'd like a one-way to Paris
Un aller-retour pour Bordeaux	A round-trip to Bordeaux
Vous avez une réduction?	Do you have a reduction?
La carte Carrissimo	A young person's card
Le train part à quelle heure?	The train leaves at what time?
A dix heures huit	At 10:08 A.M.
Quai trois	Platform 3

Sarah and Mark are in Paris en route for Bordeaux. First they take the subway, **le métro**.

They have arrived at the railway station, **la gare**, and are buying their tickets.

Find Out More

• **Un ticket** is a ticket for the subway or the bus. Otherwise it's **un billet**: **un billet de train**, **un billet de théâtre**. In the métro, it's a lot cheaper to buy a book of ten tickets: **un carnet**.
• **C'est quelle direction?** To find out how the **métro** works, see page 84.
• **La carte Carrissimo**: (for more information on traveling see *Transport* on page 82).

Over To You

1. Read the 9 sentences below. Seven of them are often said at a railway station, **à la gare**. Write G (for **gare**) in the correct boxes.

(a) **Un aller-retour pour Bordeaux.** ☐

(b) **Le train part à quelle heure?** ☐

(c) **C'est quelle direction pour la Concorde?** ☐

(d) **Le prochain train pour Paris part à huit heures dix.** ☐

(e) **Je voudrais un carnet, s'il vous plaît.** ☐

(f) **C'est quel quai, s'il vous plaît?** ☐

(g) **Deux aller pour Marseille, s'il vous plaît.** ☐

(h) **Le train part quai vingt-quatre.** ☐

(i) **Vous prenez la ligne numéro 4, direction Mairie d'Ivry.** ☐

2. Ask for one-way or round-trip tickets for the different destinations shown on the map on the next page.

LILLE
PARIS
BREST
STRASBOURG
BORDEAUX
GRENOBLE
TOULOUSE

Je voudrais un aller pour Brest.

_________________ Bordeaux.

_________________ Toulouse.

_________________ Grenoble.

_________________ Strasbourg.

_________________ Lille.

3. This conversation has gotten mixed up. Can you write it out as it should be? Try and guess who is talking and where they are.

— Oui, combien?
— Voilà, quarante francs.
— Vous prenez la ligne numéro 1.
— Donnez-moi un carnet.
— Je voudrais des tickets, s'il vous plaît.
— Oui.
— C'est direct?
— Pour la Concorde, c'est quelle direction?
— Merci, madame.

ANSWERS

1. **À la gare: a; b; d; f; g; h. c; e and i; would be heard in the subway in Paris.**
2. **Je voudrais un aller pour Bordeaux; un aller-retour pour Toulouse; un aller-retour pour Grenoble; un aller pour Strasbourg; un aller-retour pour Lille.**
3. **— Je voudrais des tickets, s'il vous plaît.**
— Oui, combien?
— Donnez-moi un carnet.
— Voilà, quarante francs.
— Pour la Concorde, c'est quelle direction?
— Vous prenez la ligne numéro 1.
— C'est direct?
— Oui.
— Merci, madame.
The people talking are a traveler and a ticket seller. They are in le métro (the underground) in Paris.

PROBLEMS

Even on vacation things can go wrong. You might lose some valuable things or get lost yourself. If you do, ask someone for the nearest police station, **le commissariat de police**. Here are a few phrases to prevent you from panicking!

KEY PHRASES

J'ai perdu mon passeport	I've lost my passport
Il est comment?	What is it like?
Il est rouge	It is red
Votre sac à dos	Your knapsack
Mon portefeuille	My wallet
C'est grave	It's serious
Je téléphone	I'll telephone
Je peux vous aider?	Can I help you?
Une amie	A (female) friend
Près du château	Near the castle
Ne vous inquiétez pas	Don't worry
Votre nom et votre adresse	Your name and your address
Vous attendez ici avec moi	You wait here with me

Sarah can't find her passport. She goes to the reception at the campsite.

Madame, j'ai perdu mon passeport.

Il est comment?

Il est rouge.

Il n'est pas dans votre sac à dos?

Non, et il n'est pas dans mon portefeuille, c'est grave!

Mais non, je téléphone au commissariat.

Mark and Sarah get separated while sightseeing one day. Mark goes to the nearest police station.

Je peux vous aider?

J'ai perdu mon ami près du château.

Ne vous inquiétez pas. Votre nom et votre adresse en France s'il vous plaît.

Kennedy. Je suis au camping.

Vous attendez ici avec moi. Je téléphone.

Find Out More

- **Il est rouge**: when referring to masculine words (**un passeport**) you'll say **il**; with feminine words (**une amie**) you will use **elle**.

Rouge is red, **bleu** is blue, **jaune** is yellow, **blanc** is white, **vert** is green (find more colors on page 63).

- **Un commissariat** is a police station in fairly large towns. In smaller places it's called **une gendarmerie**.
- **Votre nom** is your last name, but often it refers to both last name and first name.

Over To You

1. This conversation between the boy and the policeman doesn't make sense! Can you put it back in the right order?

(a) **Kennedy**
(b) **Votre adresse?**
(c) **À dix heures trente**
(d) **Où?**
(e) **J'ai perdu ma soeur.**
(f) **À quelle heure?**
(g) **Je suis au camping**
(h) **Près du château**
(i) **Votre nom, s'il vous plaît?**

2. You're telling your friend Brigitte that something is wrong.

Say you've lost your passport.

You: ______________________________

Brigitte: **Il est comment?**

Say it's red.

You: ______________________________

Brigitte: **Il n'est pas dans ton portefeuille?**

Say no, it's serious.

You: ______________________________

Brigitte: **Non, ce n'est pas grave. Regarde, il est dans ton sac à dos!**

3. Decipher this phrase and you'll feel better!

Ne vous inquiétez pas! Ce n'est pas grave.

ANSWERS

1. e; d; h; f; c; i; a; b; g. **J'ai perdu ma soeur. Où? Près du château. À quelle heure? À 10h30. Votre nom, s'il vous plaît? Kennedy. Votre adresse? Je suis au camping.**
2. **J'ai perdu mon passeport. Il est rouge. Non, c'est grave.**
3. **Ne vous inquiétez pas! Ce n'est pas grave.**

SOUVENIRS AND GIFTS

Before you leave France you'll want to buy souvenirs, **acheter des souvenirs**, and gifts, **des cadeaux**, to take back home. There are a lot of gift shops and also supermarkets, where souvenirs are usually cheaper.

KEY PHRASES

Combien coûtent les bols?	How much are the bowls?
Quarante francs le grand	40 F the big one
Trente francs le petit	30 F the small one
Vous avez des autocollants amusants?	Do you have any funny stickers?
On n'a pas de pins	We haven't got any pins (badges)
C'est trop cher	It's too expensive
Je vais prendre un stylo	I'll take a pen
Ils sont super!	They're great!
Je voudrais acheter un cadeau	I'd like to buy a present

Mark is looking for presents to take back to his parents.

Sarah is looking for an amusing present for her friend.

Find Out More

- **Un bol**: French people often drink their coffee, chocolate, or tea out of bowls rather than cups. In many shops you can buy them with a vast range of first names on them. There are very popular.
- **Combien coûtent les bols?** How much do the bowls cost? Generally **Combien ça coûte?** means *How much does it cost?*

Over To You

1. The price tags have fallen off the items in this shop window. Can you guess how much each item should cost?
For example: **Le T-shirt coûte quarante francs.**

Is this shop cheaper or more expensive than the one Mark and Sarah went to on page 49?

2. You're in a shop and you're buying souvenirs. Say hello to the lady and ask if they sell bowls.

You: ____?

Shopkeeper: **Oui. Il y a des petits et des grands.**

Ask how much they cost. Be polite, of course.

You: ____?

Shopkeeper: **Trente francs les grands, vingt francs les petits.**

Say you'll take two small bowls.

You: ____

Shopkeeper: **Et avec ça?**

Ask how much the T-shirts are.

You: ____?

Shopkeeper: **Les T-shirts coûtent 60 F ou 70 F.**

Say it's too expensive.

You: ____

3. What is Sarah asking for?

E J   A U O I V D R S   N U   E N V U S O R I   L I S   V U S O   L A P Î T

ANSWERS

1. le stylo coûte 20 F; le grand bol coûte 25 F; les autocollants coûtent 10 F; le petit bol coûte 15 F; et les pins coûtent 5 F. This shop is cheaper than the one they went to before.
2. Bonjour, madame, vous avez des bols? Combien coûtent les bols s'il vous plaît? **Je vais prendre deux petits bols.** Combien coûtent les T-shirts? C'est trop cher.
3. **Je voudrais un souvenir, s'il vous plaît.**

INVITATIONS

During your vacation, you may meet French people and be invited to their homes. Young people often meet and eat **une raclette** (a potato and cheese dish) or **des crêpes** (thin pancakes).

KEY PHRASES

Entrez	Come in
Suivez-moi	Follow me
Je vous présente mes amis	Let me introduce you to my friends
À table, tout le monde!	Dinner's ready, everyone!
On mange des crêpes	We're eating pancakes
J'adore ça!	I love it!
Donne-moi la confiture, s'il te plaît	Give me the jam please
Voilà	There you are
C'est très bon	It's very good (for food and drinks)
Tu bois du cidre ou de l'eau?	Would you like cider or water to drink?
Encore une crêpe au sucre?	Another pancake with sugar?
Elles sont excellentes	They are delicious

Mark and Sarah are invited to Arlette's house to eat pancakes with some friends.

Bonsoir Sarah, bonsoir Mark. Entrez.
Bonsoir Arlette, comment ça va?
Très bien; suivez-moi. Je vous présente mes amis anglais, Sarah et Mark.
Bonsoir, bonsoir.
À table, tout le monde!
Oh, des crêpes, j'adore ça!

Everyone is now eating.

Sarah, donne-moi la confiture, s'il te plaît.
Voilà, c'est très bon.
Du cidre, s'il te plaît.
Mark, tu bois du cidre ou de l'eau?
Sarah, encore une crêpe au sucre?
Oui, merci beaucoup. Elles sont excellentes!

Find Out More

- **Bonsoir** means good evening or goodbye at night. For the rest of the day you say **Bonjour**. You say **Bonne nuit** when you go away late at night or go off to bed.
- **Voilà** or **Tiens** is what you say when handing something over to a friend. **Tenez** is used when giving something to an adult.
- **C'est bon** means it's good, referring to food and drinks; otherwise you say **C'est bien**. **La télé**, **c'est bien**; **le cidre**, **c'est bon**.
- **S'il vous plaît** when saying **vous**, but **s'il te plaît** when saying **tu**.

Over To You

1. Unravel what each person is saying. For example:

2. Find the missing words in the dialogue. The drawings will help you.

(a) **À ______ tout le monde!**
(b) **Oh, des ________ j'adore ça!**
(c) **Mark, donne-moi la __________, s'il te plaît.**
(d) **Tu bois du ______ ou de l'______ ?**
(e) **Du ______, s'il te plaît.**

3. You're invited to your friend's house for dinner. Circle the words and phrases you need.

— Bonsoir — Bonjour — Au revoir.
— Comment ça va? — C'est combien?
— Les crêpes sont excellentes — Je vous présente les crêpes — Les crêpes sont mes amies.
— C'est bon — C'est bien — C'est à table.

ANSWERS

1. **Comment ça va? Suivez-moi. À table! J'adore les crêpes.**
2. **(a) table (b) crêpes (c) confiture (d) cidre, eau (e) cidre.**
3. **Bonsoir. Comment ça va? Les crêpes sont excellentes. C'est bon.**

USEFUL WORDS AND PHRASES

PLACES *(les lieux — m)*

une gare	railway station
un musée	museum
une église	church
un piéton	pedestrian
une rue piétonne	pedestrian precinct
une piscine	swimming-pool
c'est loin / c'est près	it's far / it's near
au bout de la rue	at the end of the street
en face de la poste	across from the post office
après / avant les feux	after / before the traffic lights
devant / derrière	in front of / behind
à cinq minutes d'ici	five minutes away from here
descendez la rue	go down the street
fermé / ouvert	closed / open
un plan	map

EATING AND DRINKING *(manger et boire)*

un petit déjeuner	breakfast
un déjeuner	lunch
un dîner	dinner
un jus de pomme	apple juice
un jus d'orange	orange juice
une glace à la fraise	strawberry ice cream
une glace au chocolat / à la vanille	chocolate / vanilla ice cream
j'ai faim	I'm hungry
j'ai soif	I'm thirsty
un sandwich au fromage	cheese sandwich
un croque-madame	toasted ham and cheese sandwich with a fried egg on top
une salade verte	green salad
un pain au chocolat	chocolate filled roll
une salade niçoise	tuna fish salad
une saucisse	sausage

TRAVEL *(les voyages — m)*

une voiture	car
un arrêt d'autobus	bus stop
une gare routière	coach station
un horaire	timetable
un billet	train ticket
le nord/le sud/l'est/ l'ouest	north/south/east/ west
première classe	first class
deuxième classe	second class
une place réservée	reserved seat
une voiture (d'un train)	train car
une correspondance	connection, change
l'arrivée *(f)*	arrival
le départ	departure
une voie	platform
un quai	platform
un voyage	trip, journey
c'est libre?	is it free?
c'est occupé?/c'est réservé?	is it occupied/is it reserved?

ACCOMMODATION *(l'hébergement — m)*

écrire	to write
un prénom	first name
une adresse	address
une date de naissance	date of birth
un lieu de naissance	place of birth
une nationalité	nationality
une profession	profession
une clé	key
une salle de bains	bathroom
complet	full
les bagages *(m)*	luggage
une prise	socket
une lumière	light
ça ne marche pas	it doesn't work
il y a du bruit	it's noisy
ce n'est pas propre	it isn't clean

RELATIVES AND FRIENDS *(la famille et les amis — f, m)*

les parents *(m)*	parents
une mère	mother
un père	father
un oncle	uncle
une tante	aunt
un cousin/une cousine	(male) cousin/(female) cousin
une famille	family
un ami	(male) friend
une amie	(female) friend
un petit ami	boy friend
une petite amie	girl friend

SPARE TIME *(les loisirs — m)*

la musique classique	classical music
la musique pop	pop music
un chanteur	male singer
une chanteuse	female singer
un acteur/une actrice	actor/actress
une vedette	star
gratuit	free
payant	not free
une fête	party, festival
une pièce de théâtre	play
jouer	to play
aimer	to like
se baigner	to go swimming
lire	to read

POST AND TELEPHONE *(la poste et le téléphone)*

envoyer	to send
poster	to mail
un paquet	package
introduire la carte	to insert the card
fermer le volet	to close the flap
numéroter	to dial the number
retirer la carte	to take out the card
patienter	to wait

HEALTH *(la santé)*

une température	temperature
une insolation	sunstroke
une piqûre	sting, injection
une rage de dents	toothache
un hôpital	hospital
un médicament	medicine
une ordonnance	prescription
je ne me sens pas bien	I don't feel well
les règles *(f)*	periods
le sang	blood
un cabinet (de consultation)	doctor's surgery
le service des urgences	emergency room
c'est urgent	it's urgent
je me suis brûlé(e)	I've burned myself
je me suis cassé . . .	I've broken . . .
j'ai mal à . . .	I've got pain . . .
avaler	to swallow
une fois par jour	once a day
un antibiotique	antibiotic
un sirop	syrup

SHOPPING *(les courses — f)*

un fruit	fruit
une cerise	cherry
une fraise	strawberry
un citron	lemon
le raisin	grapes
un concombre	cucumber
le pain	bread
le lait	milk
le beurre	butter
la crème	cream
le sucre	sugar
la farine	flour
un œuf	egg
la viande	meat
le poisson	fish
une boîte de conserve	can of something
un produit surgelé	frozen food
un bonbon	candy
un biscuit	biscuit
une pizza	pizza
la pâtisserie	pastries
un disque	record
un disque compact	CD
une cassette	cassette
un livre	book
les lunettes de soleil *(f)*	sunglasses
les vêtements *(m)*	clothes
une veste	jacket
une chemise	shirt
un sac	bag
un porte-monnaie	purse
un porte-clés	key ring
en plastique	plastic
en cuir	leather
l'argent	money
c'est plus cher	it's more expensive
c'est moins cher	it's less expensive
il y a un défaut	there's something wrong with it
je voudrais échanger	I'd like to exchange

WEATHER *(le temps)*

quel temps fait-il?	what's the weather like?
il fait beau	it's nice
il fait chaud	it's hot
il fait mauvais	it's nasty
il fait froid	it's cold
il fait frais	it's cool
il fait humide	it's wet
il pleut	it's raining
il neige	it's snowing

NUMBERS *(les nombres — m)*

0	zéro	
1	un	premier
2	deux	deuxième, second(e)
3	trois	troisième
4	quatre	quatrième
5	cinq	cinquième
6	six	sixième
7	sept	septième
8	huit	huitième
9	neuf	neuvième
10	dix	dixième
11	onze	onzième
12	douze	douzième
13	treize	treizième
14	quatorze	quatorzième
15	quinze	quinzième
16	seize	seizième
17	dix-sept	dix-septième
18	dix-huit	dix-huitième
19	dix-neuf	dix-neuvième
20	vingt	vingtième
21	vingt-et-un	vingt-et-unième
22	vingt-deux	vingt-deuxième
23	vingt-trois	vingt-troisième
30	trente	trentième
31	trente-et-un	trente-et-unième
32	trente-deux	trente-deuxième
40	quarante	quarantième
50	cinquante	cinquantième
60	soixante	soixantième
70	soixante-dix	soixante-dixième
71	soixante-et-onze	soixante-et-onzième
80	quatre-vingts	quatre-vingtième
81	quatre-vingt-un	quatre-vingt-unième
90	quatre-vingt-dix	quatre-vingt-dixième
91	quatre-vingt-onze	quatre-vingt-onzième
100	cent	centième

200	deux cents	deux centième
1000	mille	millième
10 000	dix mille	dix millième

1/2 **un demi** 1/5 **un cinquième** 1/6 **un sixième**
1/4 **un quart** 1/3 **un tiers**

DAYS AND MONTHS *(les jours — m et les mois — m)*

Les jours (m) **de la semaine**		**The days of the week**	
lundi	Monday	**vendredi**	Friday
mardi	Tuesday	**samedi**	Saturday
mercredi	Wednesday	**dimanche**	Sunday
jeudi	Thursday	**le dimanche**	On Sundays

Les mois (m) **de l'année** (f)		**The months of the year**	
janvier	January	**juillet**	July
février	February	**août**	August
mars	March	**septembre**	September
avril	April	**octobre**	October
mai	May	**novembre**	November
juin	June	**décembre**	December

TIME *(l'heure — f)*

Quelle heure est-il? What's the time?

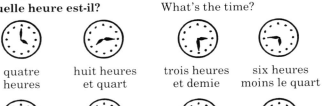

quatre heures — huit heures et quart

trois heures et demie

six heures moins le quart

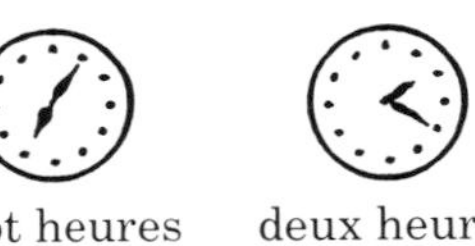

sept heures cinq — deux heures vingt

cinq heures moins vingt-cinq

six heures moins dix

midi

00·00 minuit

When it's 1 A.M., 2 A.M., 3 A.M., 4 A.M., 5 A.M., and 6 A.M., you say **1 heure du matin**, **deux heures du matin**, etc.

COLORS *(les couleurs — f)*

bleu(e)	blue	**rose**	pink
blanc(he)	white	**noir(e)**	black
rouge	red	**marron**	brown
jaune	yellow	**violet(te)**	purple
orange	orange	**gris(e)**	grey
vert(e)	green	**beige**	beige

CLOTHES SIZES *(la taille des vêtements)*

Quelle est votre taille? What's your size?

Shirts, T-shirts, sweaters, etc., are all marked S, M, L, XL, just as in the US. The sizes are exactly the same. However, dresses and skirts do have equivalent sizes and so do shoes. Here are some tables to show them:

Girls' Clothes

US	France
8	36
10	38
12	40
14	42
16	44

Shoes

US	France
6	36
7	37
8	38
9	39
10	40

MONEY *(l'argent — m)*

un billet	bill
une pièce de monnaie	coin
la monnaie	change
un franc	franc
un centime	centime

WEIGHTS AND MEASURES *(les poids — m et les mesures — f)*

une livre	pound
une demi-livre	half a pound
un kilo	kilo
un litre	liter
un demi-litre	half a liter
un mètre	meter

USEFUL SLANG EXPRESSIONS

une bagnole	car	**hyper**	really
une baraque	house	**un mec / un type**	guy
une boîte	disco	**une nana**	girl
un boulot	job	**peinard/cool**	cool
une boum	party	**une piaule**	bedroom
un bouquin	book	**un pieu**	bed
branché	with it	**relax**	relaxed
un cinoche	cinema	**un resto**	restaurant
dingue	mad	**sympa**	nice
un flic	policeman	**zut!**	darn!
le fric	money		
glander	to loiter		

bouffer; je bouffe	to eat; I'm eating
ça craint	it's bad
ça me rase	it's boring
c'est bourré	it's full
c'est chouette	it's great
être à la bourre	to be in a hurry
être bourré	to be drunk
j'ai la crève	I've got a cold
j'en ai marre	I'm fed up
je n'ai pas un rond	I'm broke
je suis crevé / KO	I'm very tired
les Amerloques	Americans
prendre un pot	to have a drink
rigoler; je rigole	to laugh; I'm laughing
s'éclater; je m'éclate	to have a good time; I'm having a good time
se marrer; je me marre	to laugh, to have fun; I'm laughing; I'm having fun

FRANCE
AND
THE FRENCH

BELGIQUE
LA MANCHE
LILLE
LUXEMBOURG
ALLEMAGNE
PARIS
Seine
STRASBOURG
NANCY
Les Vosges
Rhin
Loire
DIJON
NANTES
LE JURA
SUISSE
OCEAN
ATLANTIQUE
CLERMONT
FERRAND
LYON
LE
MASSIF
CENTRAL
BORDEAUX
Rhône
LES ALPES
ITALIE
La Garonne
TOULOUSE
MARSEILLE
LES PYRENEES
ESPAGNE
MER MÉDITERRANÉE

FRANCE AND THE FRENCH

Life in France

France is the second largest country in the European Community (EC). It's twice the size of Great Britain. It's surrounded by six countries: Belgium, Luxembourg, Germany, Switzerland, Italy and Spain, and three seas: the English Channel (**la Manche**), the Atlantic Ocean (**l'Océan Atlantique**) and the Mediterranean Sea (**la mer Méditerranée**). It has five mountain ranges: **les Vosges**, **le Jura**, **les Alpes**, **les Pyrénées** and **le Massif Central**, and five main rivers: **la Seine**, **la Loire**, **la Garonne**, **le Rhône** and **le Rhin**.

France has about 56 million inhabitants. Paris, the capital, is the largest city with ten million people in the city and the suburbs (**la banlieue**). The main towns are **Lyon** and **Marseille**, then **Lille**, **Strasbourg**, **Nantes**, **Bordeaux**, **Toulouse**, **Clermont-Ferrand**, **Nancy**, and **Dijon**.

France is divided into 21 regions which are very different from each other, with different scenery, food, customs, and accents.

France is a republic and has a president (**le Président de la République**) who is elected for seven years. The motto of the republic is Freedom, Equality, Fraternity: **Liberté, Égalité, Fraternité**. The President lives and works in

NORD-PAS-DE-CALAIS
PICARDIE
NORMANDIE
Paris
ILE DE FRANCE
CHAMPAGNE-ARDENNE
LORRAINE-VOSGES-ALSACE
BRETAGNE
PAYS DE LA LOIRE
CENTRE
Dijon
FRANCHE-COMTÉ
BOURGOGNE
POITOU-CHARENTES
Lyon
RHÔNE-ALPES
LIMOUSIN
Bordeaux
AUVERGNE
Montélimar
AQUITAINE
PROVENCE-ALPES-CÔTE D'AZUR
Nice
MIDI PYRÉNÉES
LANGUEDOC-ROUSSILLON
Cavaillon
Toulouse
Marseille
RIVIERA CÔTE D'AZUR
Bayonne

l'Élysée near the Champs-Élysées.

France is divided into 95 departments which include an island, Corsica (**la Corse**), and four overseas departments: **la Guadeloupe**, **la Martinique**, **la Guyane**, and **la Réunion**.

The departments are listed in alphabetical order from 01 (**Ain**) to 90 (**territoire de Belfort**). The five departments around Paris representing the suburbs are 91, 92, 93, 94, and 95.

When writing a letter you use the department number as a postal code in front of the name of the town: 69000 Lyon; 13000 Marseille.

The two last figures on car license plates are the number of the department. You can tell where a car comes from: 1340 MXY 75 is a car registered in Paris (department of the *Seine*).

Over To You

Looking at the map opposite link the following food with the town or region they come from.

1. **le camembert**	a. **Montélimar**
2. **la moutarde**	b. **Nice**
3. **les escargots**	c. **Cavaillon**
4. **les crêpes**	d. **Normandie**
5. **les melons**	e. **Alsace**
6. **la choucroute**	f. **Dijon**
7. **la salade niçoise**	g. **Lyon**
8. **le jambon**	h. **Bourgogne**
9. **le nougat**	i. **Bayonne**
10. **les saucisses**	j. **Bretagne**

ANSWERS

1d; 2f; 3h; 4j; 5c; 6e; 7b; 8i; 9a; 10g.

TOURIST FRANCE

During your travels you will meet many French people, and some of them will be on vacation themselves. Everyone in France has five weeks' paid vacation, and 59% of them stay in their own country. They usually travel in August or they go skiing in the Alps or the Pyrenees in the winter. Here are postcards from some of their favorite places. Perhaps you'll want to visit one yourself.

Of course, we'll start with Paris, the capital city. The center of Paris, **l'Ile de la Cité**, has the shape of a boat. This has led to the city's motto—it floats but never sinks. You can also see the cathedral of **Notre-Dame**, and the **Louvre** museum, which used to be the king's palace.

The Eiffel Tower was built by **Monsieur Eiffel** at the end of the nineteenth century. A visit to the top will give you a splendid view of the city.

The Pompidou Center at **Beaubourg** is bright blue and looks like a factory with all its pipes on the outside. It has a library, a museum, and regularly shows films—outside it has become a center for street musicians, painters, clowns, and singers. Nearby you will find **Les Halles**, which is a big shopping mall and park.

Do not miss a walk along the **Champs-Elysées** between the **Louvre** and the **Arc de Triomphe** through the **Place de la Concorde**. But be warned that anything bought in this area will be very expensive.

A very relaxing way to see Paris is to take a boat ride from the Eiffel Tower to the **Ile St Louis**, these boats are called the **bateaux mouches**.

A few miles outside Paris is **Versailles**, the castle of Louis XIV. It is a beautiful palace, with a fabulously rich interior and magnificent gardens with lakes and fountains. It is very nice to rent bikes here and ride around the park. There will probably be lines to get into **Versailles**, but don't worry, it's well worth the wait.

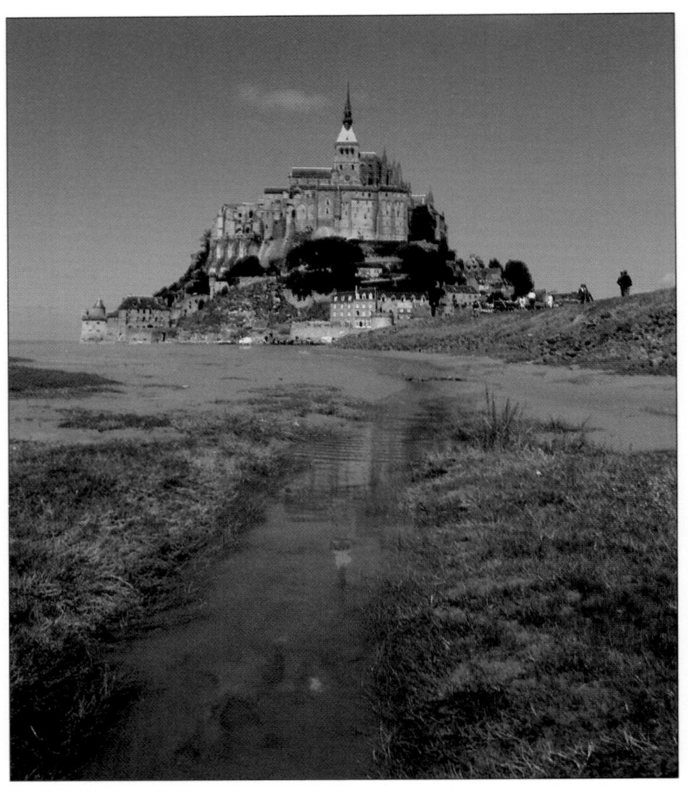

West of Paris, in Normandy, you will find **Mont St Michel**. This is the most visited monument in France, and well worth a visit. But watch out, it is surrounded by the sea at high tide! Its medieval abbey and churches have been called **la merveille** (the marvel). Further west is Brittany, also famous for its beaches, where you can swim, sail, surf or just take the sun. It is also full of pretty villages, and is famous for its pancakes.

To the southwest of Paris, near Tours, are **les châteaux de la Loire**. This is a collection of sixteenth-century castles built by the kings of France. The most famous are the **Chenonceaux**, **Amboise**, **Azay-le-Rideau**, **Blois**, **Chambord**, **Le Lude**, and **Ussé**.

Southeast of the capital is **Chamonix**, in the Alps near Switzerland. This is France's most popular ski resort. But even if you don't ski it is still worth

a summer visit. There are a vast range of outdoor activities to be had here: hiking, sailing, swimming, and so on.

The southeast coast of France is called the **Côte d'Azur**. This is the country's warmest region. Its resorts are famous because they are **Nice!** and because they attract the stars. **St. Tropez**, **Cannes**, and **St. Raphaël** are all beautiful places, but in the summer they are often too full of beautiful people!

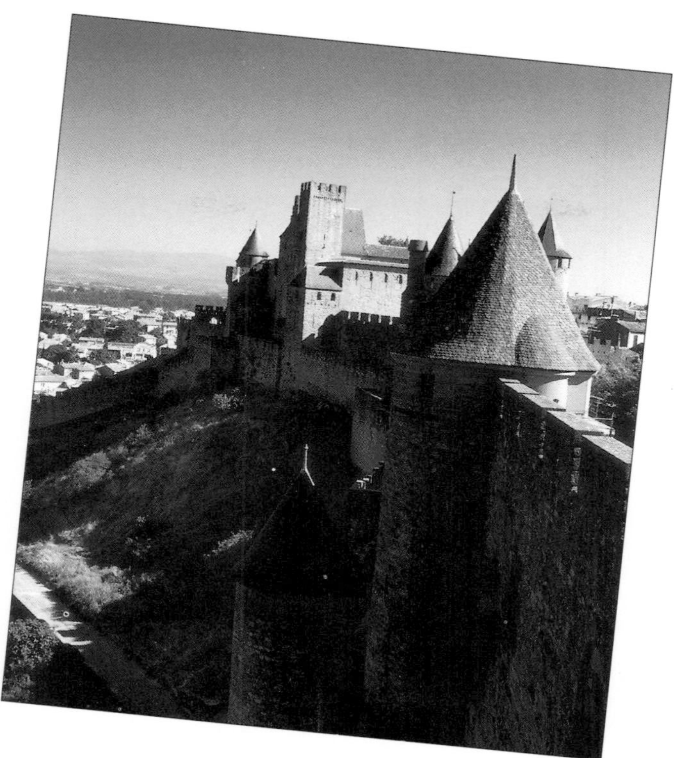

In the southwest stands **Carcassonne**. Next to the modern town you will find a medieval walled city, with streets, shops, and a castle. In summer you may need to remember your umbrella, as it is very hot during July and August.

Please remember we have only mentioned a few places for you to visit in this book. France has 21 regions and each is famous for its different tourist attractions.

Over To You

Looking at the drawings below, find the names of the regions in which you can find the interesting places shown.

ANSWERS

Paris; Provence-Côte d'Azur; Basse-Normandie; Languedoc-Roussillon.

Travelers' Information

SIGNS *(les panneaux — m)*

When you arrive in France you might want to understand the signs you see in the street. Here are a few.

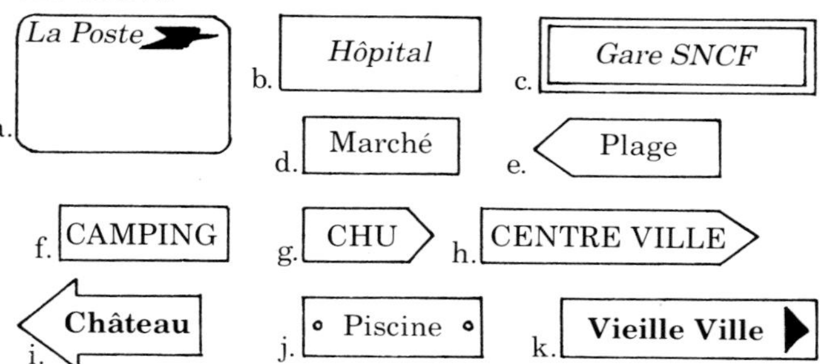

a. post office, b. hospital, c. railway station, d. market, e. beach, f. camping, g. CHU, usually a big city hospital, h. downtown, i. castle, j. swimming pool, k. old town

BANKS *(les banques — f)*

They are usually open from 9 A.M. to 4:30 or 5:00 P.M. in large towns. They close between noon and 2 P.M. elsewhere.

Not many small banks change money and you'll often see the "no change" sign. However, they'll direct you to a bank or to a **Bureau de Change** that does change money.
Most of them cash travelers cheques (**les chèques de voyages**), so if you have these in Francs, it's very easy.
The main banks are **la BNP**, **Crédit Lyonnais** and **le Crédit Agricole**.

POST OFFICES *(les postes — f)*

They are usually open from 8 A.M. to 7 P.M. in large towns. They are closed between midday and 2 P.M. in smaller places and close earlier in the evening at 5 or 6 P.M.
You can buy stamps and send letters or packages at the counter called: **Lettres et paquets – Affranchissements** (letters and packages).
You can avoid waiting by weighing your letter on the automatic yellow machine in the post office.
You can buy your stamps from an automatic machine. At another counter, **Change/télécarte**, you can change money and buy a phonecard.
There are mailboxes in the street. They are yellow.
When mailing a letter, send it to **autres destinations** (other destinations) or **étranger** (abroad).
To save time and avoid waiting when you just want to buy some stamps, go to a tobacco shop.

TOBACCO SHOPS *(les tabacs — m)*

They are very useful shops since you can buy many other articles than cigarettes: stamps, phonecards, postcards, candy, subway tickets, chocolate, chewing gum, etc. They are also open longer hours since many **tabacs** are also **cafés**.

CAFES *(les cafés— m)*

They are a meeting point for young people. You can have a drink and stay as long as you wish: no one will hassle you to have another drink. Young people sit together and chat, do their homework, or have a snack. In a café you can also play tabletop soccer (**le babyfoot**), or try out a pinball machine (**le flipper**) or video games (**les jeux vidéo**), or listen to records on the juke box (**le juke box**).

The cheapest way to buy a drink is to have it at the bar. It's a bit more expensive sitting inside, and more expensive still on a terrace. The 15% service charge is included. The waiter will bring your bill with your order. If you're in a hurry and the waiter is busy, you can leave the exact amount on the table and go.

If you're very thirsty you can always ask for a pitcher of water (**une carafe d'eau**) with your drink. It's free.

Nothing alcoholic will be served to people under 16 years of age.

If you need to go to the restroom (**les toilettes**), you ask: **Où sont les toilettes?**

TRANSPORT *(le transport)*

1. **Trains (les trains)** are run by the SNCF, the French national rail service.

You'll most likely travel on an orange train, **un train corail**, or on **le TGV, Train à Grande Vitesse** (high speed train): it's orange for the

South and East and blue for the Atlantic coast. The TGV costs the same price as ordinary trains but on some you have to pay an extra fee and you must have a reserved seat. If you get the chance, try it and you'll speed along at between 150 and 180 miles per hour!

To buy a ticket you can wait at a counter, **un guichet banlieue** (for the suburbs) or **grandes lignes** (for national and international lines).

If you are in a hurry you can use a credit card or coins to get a ticket from a computer ticket machine (**la billetterie**).

If you're between 12 and 25 years old you can purchase the card **Carrissimo** that enables you and up to three of your friends to travel at reduced fares.

With this card, you can get lower prices when travelling off-peak: 50% in the blue period or 20% in the white period.

Find out which platform, **quai** or **voie**, your train leaves from and get there ahead of time. Remember, French trains run on time, so don't leave things to the last moment.

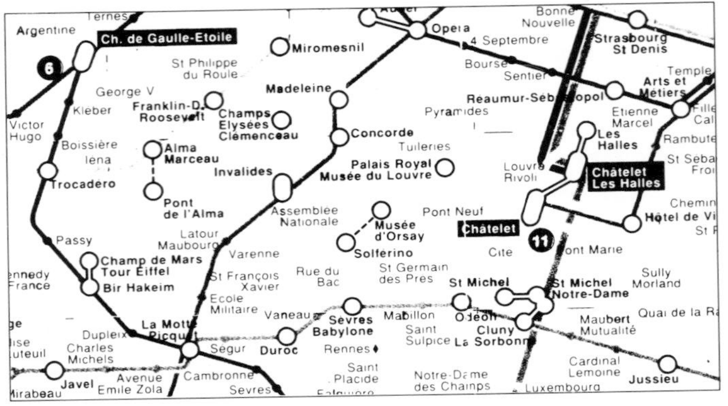

2. **The underground (le métro)** can be used in Paris, Lyon and Marseille.

Buy tickets in books of ten (**un carnet**) which is cheaper than buying tickets separately.

You can also get cheap daily passes and a weekly or monthly card, **la carte orange**.

With one ticket you can go anywhere. Trains run every two minutes and the stations are close to one another.

To find your way on the métro map, look for the line you want (it has a number) and for the direction (the name of the last station). When changing station (**quand vous changez**), look for the sign **correspondances**. In each métro station there is a map (**un plan**).

The métro runs from 5:15 A.M. to 12:45 A.M.

The RER (**réseau express régional**, fast trains going far in the Paris suburbs) uses fast trains which enable you to get to and from suburbs very quickly. You can travel on it with the same tickets you use for the métro when traveling inside Paris.

3. **Buses and coaches (les bus et les cars — m)** are the best way to visit a town or a region. Don't be afraid to go on a bus for fear of missing your stop. Drivers are very helpful if asked: **Vous pourrez m'indiquer l'arrêt x?** (Could you tell me when we get to stop x?) There is also a map of the bus route at the bus stop and in the bus.
In Paris bus tickets are the same as métro tickets. The maximum charge for a ride is two tickets. It's cheaper to buy tickets from métro stations or tobacco shops before you get on the bus. When visiting small places that aren't on a train line, you go to the coach station, **la gare routière**, to get a coach, **un car**. You ask for a one-way or a round-trip ticket. Inquire about day trip discounts. When getting on a bus or a coach, don't forget to stamp your ticket in a machine (**le composteur**) next to the driver, if there is one, except for the **carte orange** ticket, which you just need to show to the driver.
In many towns, day trips are organized: it's a cheap and comfortable way of exploring a town or a region. Sometimes there is a guide in the coach who might even speak English!

TELEPHONES *(les téléphones — m)*

Most public phones work with an electronic card, **une télécarte**, and don't take coins. You can buy a card at tabacs, post offices, newspaper shops, big stores, and in any shop that has this sign:

You can buy 50 unit cards (**50 unités**) for 40 F or 120 units (**120 unités**) for 96 F.

Most phone booths have instructions in English explaining how to use the card. At the end of your call you will hear a “bip, bip” sound to remind you not to forget your card. When you phone, you’ll see some words in a small screen:

DÉCROCHEZ (lift the receiver),
INTRODUIRE LA CARTE (insert the card),
OU FAITES LE NUMÉRO D’URGENCE (or dial the emergency number – it is free).
FERMEZ LE VOLET (close the flap), **CRÉDIT 40,20 F** (your credit on the card is 40,20 F),
NUMÉROTEZ (dial), **PATIENTEZ** (hold on),
NUMÉRO APPELÉ 45844681 (number called 45844681). While talking you can check how many francs or units you have left. When your conversation is over, you will see **CRÉDIT X F** or **X Unités**.
RACCROCHEZ (put the receiver back),
RETIREZ VOTRE CARTE (remove your card).

To call the U.S., first dial 19, wait for a dial tone, then dial 1 + your area code and phone number.

For example, your phone number is 708-555-1719. From France, you dial: 19-1-708-555-1719. Here are some useful numbers:

12 information (**renseignements**)
18 emergencies and fire department (**urgence - pompiers**)
17 police (**police**)

It's much cheaper to phone on weekdays after 9:30 P.M., on Saturdays after 2 P.M., or anytime on Sundays.
You might still find coin phones in small towns, They take 5, 2 or 1 F coins, but are often out of order.
In restaurants, cafés and sportsclubs, you may see a small white portable phone booth: **point phone**. This works with 1 F coins.

MINITELS *(m)*

When you are in someone's house or in a post office, you can look up phone numbers in the Minitel, a popular computer service, by dialing 11. This will give you access to any phone number in France. The service is free for the first three minutes. Minitels offer other services which you have to pay for (on the phone bill): information about trains, boats or planes, tickets, sports events, music, theater, etc.

MUSEUMS *(les musées — m)*

All over France, museums are closed on Tuesdays, but you may find some are closed on Mondays, so check before you go. Admission is usually free on

Sundays, and many have discounts then. Bilingual brochures or English commentaries on cassettes are very often available.
The most famous museum in Paris is **le Louvre**: inside you can admire **la Joconde**, the Mona Lisa, by Leonardo da Vinci, probably the most famous painting in the world.
No wonder she's smiling!

COMICS *(les bandes dessinées — f)*

Une BD (bande dessinée) is a very good way to improve your French!
The most famous are **Astérix**, **Lucky Luke**, **Tintin** and **les Schtroumpfs**, known in English-speaking countries as Smurfs.
You can also go to the public library and borrow books. Many have comics translated into English!

NEWSPAPERS *(les journaux — m)*

They can be found at the newsagent **la Maison de la Presse** or in newsstands on the street (**les kiosques**).
There are many magazines for young people among which are: **Okapi**, **Mikado**, and **le Journal des Jeunes**.

TV AND RADIO *(la télé et la radio)*

There are six TV channels **TF1**, **France 2**, **France 3**, **Canal+** (to subscribers only), **ARTE**, and **M6**. The main radio stations are **France Inter**, **RTL**, and **Europe 1**. You can also hear pop music non-stop on many local stations (**les radios libres**): **NRJ** (which sounds like energy when you say it), **Fun FM**, and **Skyrock** are also very popular.

SHOPS *(les magasins — m)*

They are usually open between 9 A.M. and 7 P.M. in large towns. In other places they are open from 9 A.M. to noon and from 2 P.M. to 7 P.M. Food shops, except for supermarkets, are open from 7 A.M. to 1 P.M. and from 4 P.M. to 8 P.M. so you can go out and buy your **baguette** at 7 A.M.! Supermarkets and hypermarkets are generally to be found on the edge of towns; they are open from 9 A.M. to 8 P.M., sometimes to 10 P.M. Local markets take place once or twice a week from 8 A.M. to 1 P.M. They are very popular and you'll be able to buy any food you want, as well as clothes. Do not miss a visit to a cheese shop: There are 365 cheeses (**fromages**) in France, as many as there are days in a year!

Since most food shops are open on Sundays until 1 P.M., they are usually closed on Mondays or on another day of the week.

Department stores (**les grands magasins**) are to be found in large towns: **le Printemps, les Galeries Lafayette** or **les Nouvelles Galeries**. They are pleasant to shop in and you can find nearly everything there (except for food), but they are quite expensive. You can go to cheaper stores, like **Monoprix** or **Prisunic**, which you will find in most towns. When buying clothes, try the sales (**les soldes**) from the end of June to the end of August and after Christmas. You can then buy clothes and shoes at half price. Small shops are usually cheaper than department stores.

It is normal for salespeople to come and ask you what you need as soon as you go in: **Je peux vous aider?** (Can I help you?). It is the custom in France for salespeople to look after the public with great care, so feel free to say that you're just looking: **Je regarde, merci**.

However, if you want to try on some clothes ask, **Je peux essayer?** You'll be directed to a fitting-room, **une cabine**.

When buying a present, **un cadeau**, you can ask the clerk in any shop to wrap it up for you: **Je voudrais un paquet-cadeau**.

If you want to give someone flowers, avoid chrysanthemums, associated in France with graveyards! You can find ready-made **bouquets** outside flower shops: these are pretty and cheap. Tell the clerk it's to give to someone: **C'est pour offrir**. You will get a very attractive wrapping. You should know that when you offer red roses, this means that you are declaring your love to the person who will receive them!

LEISURE *(les loisirs — m)*

Nearly every town has sports fields and tennis courts, so young people can practice after school and on weekends: football, judo, tennis and athletics.

There are also local youth centers, **les Maisons des Jeunes et de la Culture**, known as **MJC**. They offer a wide range of activities from sports to dance, drama, weaving, music, yoga, etc. Young people go there mainly on Wednesdays and Saturdays – because there is no school in the afternoons.

At home, young people spend quite a lot of time watching television, playing card games (**les cartes**) and board games (**les jeux de société**). They also read comics (**les BD**) and listen to music on CDs (**les compacts** or **les CD**) or on their Walkman (**le baladeur**).

At night, young people go and have a drink in a café, or eat a pizza or pancakes. They also go to the movies. Discos open at around 10:30 P.M. and are quite expensive, so, only older people (from 18 years on) go to them. Also, French parents are quite strict, and young people under 18 don't go out late at night, especially during school terms.

Sunday is the peak time for leisure activities. People go out to visit their families (grandparents, aunts and uncles), go to a restaurant, to sports matches, to the movies, or out for a walk. When they stay at home, they have the biggest lunch of the week, with the traditional roast and cakes: **un rôti et des gâteaux**.

SCHOOL *(l'école — f)*

In France if you're between ages 11 and 16 you go to a secondary school (**un collège**). After that, you go to **un lycée** (a high school). School starts early in September and gets out early in July. Students have a ten day break every six weeks. They study one foreign language in sixth grade (**la sixième**), usually English (**l'anglais**) or German (**l'allemand**). They choose a second foreign language two years later:
German, English, Spanish or Italian. Some also study Latin or Greek.

School is from 8:30 A.M. to 5:00 P.M., but it can vary, depending on the schedule. There is school on Saturday mornings, but there is a lot of pressure from parents to stop this so that everyone can enjoy the weekend, **le week-end**! All students go to the swimming pool and learn to swim as it's part of the graduation exam (**le bac**). On the whole, however, they spend much less time on sports at school in France than in other countries. At night they spend a minimum of two hours on their homework.

HEALTH *(la santé)*

In an emergency, go to the nearest hospital, to the emergency room (**le service des urgences**). Otherwise go to any pharmacy (**la pharmacie**): you can easily find one, with a green cross outside. They'll be able to give you the name of a doctor and even call one for you. They're open between 9 A.M. and 7 P.M., some until 8 P.M. If you have a problem at night or on the weekend, go to the nearest pharmacy: in the window there will be a list of the pharmacists who are on duty 24 hours a day (**les pharmacies de garde**) and the doctors who are on duty (**les médecins de garde**) in the area. When you go to the doctor, or to the hospital, you'll have to pay, but you'll be given a National Health form (**une feuille de maladie**) which should enable you to get reimbursed when you return home. You can also stick on it the price tags (**les vignettes)** from the medicine boxes that you get from the pharmacist. You may be able to get reimbursed by your insurance company.

TRAFFIC *(la circulation)*

Watch out in France when crossing streets as drivers tend to go very fast, stop at the very last minute at traffic lights, and ignore pedestrian crossings.

GREETINGS *(saluer)*

When you meet a friend, or someone you know quite well, it is normal to kiss him or her on the cheeks twice, three times . . . even four times in some parts of France. Don't feel embarrassed, and do it as many times as they do!

When meeting someone you don't know at all, or not too well, you shake hands. When greeting strangers in a shop or a café it is always more polite to say **Bonjour Monsieur** or **Bonjour Madame** than **Bonjour** on its own.

MANNERS *(les manières)*

When you stay with a family:

— if someone sneezes you say: **À tes/vos souhaits!** (Bless you!)

— if it's your friend's name day, you say: **Bonne fête!**

— if you want to leave the table, you ask: **Je peux sortir de table?**

— if you want to help: **Je peux vous aider?**

— if you have had enough to eat always say first that it was good, as food is quite an important thing to French people, and then that you have had enough: **C'était très bon, mais j'ai assez mangé**.

— to be polite put both hands on the table during meals.

LA RECETTE DES CRÊPES

To make delicious pancakes, young French people's favorite food, you'll need the following: **4 oeufs** (4 eggs); **250 g de farine** (½ pound of flour); **un demi-litre de lait** (1 pint of milk); **un quart de litre d'eau** (½ pint of water). Beat the ingredients together, and leave to stand for an hour or so. Then cook as normal pancakes.

FRENCH: A WORLD LANGUAGE

Here is a map of different countries where French is spoken. You'll notice that French is spoken in many African countries. About 75 million people have French as their native language, and over 200 million are French-speaking.

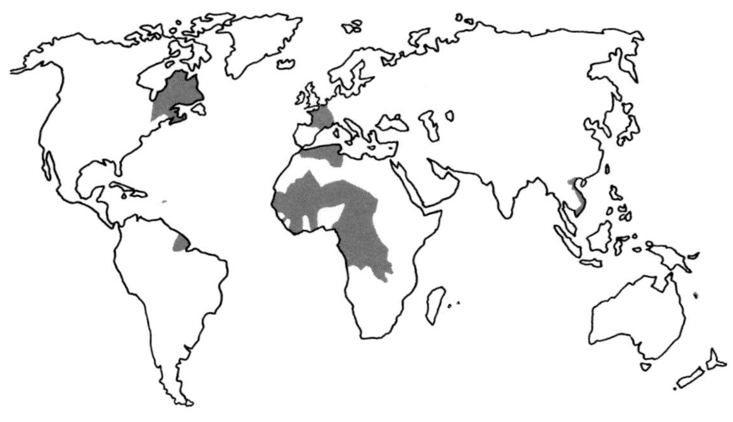

Over To You

Here is a list of some countries. Using your atlas and the map on page 95 cross out the ones where French is not spoken.

Tunisie; Belgique; Allemagne; Sénégal; Vietnam; Nouvelle-Calédonie; Nouvelle-Zélande; Niger; Tchad; Québec; Réunion; Portugal; Mali; Martinique; Australie; Île Maurice; Chili; Égypte; Gabon; Écosse.

ANSWERS

Allemagne; Nouvelle-Zélande; Portugal, Australie; Chili; Égypte; Écosse.